a smart girl's guide
to the
internet

how to connect with friends,
find what you need,
and stay safe online

by Sharon Cindrich

illustrated by
Ali Douglass

★ American Girl®

Published by American Girl Publishing, Inc.
Copyright © 2009 by American Girl, LLC

Questions or comments? Call 1-800-845-0005,
visit our Web site at americangirl.com, or write to Customer Service,
American Girl, 8400 Fairway Place, Middleton, WI 53562.

Printed in China
09 10 11 12 13 14 15 16 LEO 10 9 8 7 6 5 4 3 2 1

Editorial Development: Erin Falligant
Art Direction and Design: Lisa Wilber, Chris Lorette David
Production: Tami Kepler, Sarah Boecher, Jeannette Bailey,
Judith Lary
Illustrations: Ali Douglass

Special thanks to The Ophelia Project

Dear Reader,

Playing games, finding homework help, and sending e-mails are just a few of the things girls like you do online every day. It's easy to get on the Internet and easy to get what you need, right?

Maybe. But staying *safe* online takes practice and some skills. This book will give you the tools you need to be a smart Internet user. Quizzes and "What do you do?" scenarios help you figure out what information you should never share online—and what to do if a cyberbully targets you.

You'll also find ideas for how to get the most out of your time online. Learn e-mail do's and don'ts, practice net lingo, and express yourself with emoticons and personalized e-mail messages. Have fun with digital photos, music, and movies, and find out how—and when it's O.K.—to share them online.

Do your parents have rules about using the Internet? Most parents do. Those rules are meant to protect you. Be patient, and follow the tips in this book to show your parents that you can be responsible online. Visit "Fun for Girls" at **americangirl.com** to find a printable Internet contract, plus quizzes and other activities from *A Smart Girl's Guide to the Internet*.

The Internet is always changing and growing. We hope this book helps you grow and learn right along with it.

Your friends at American Girl

contents

your life online

Start up. Log on. Click. You're on the Internet—a connection to your friends, your school, and your world. You may not think too much about e-mailing friends or doing school research online, but the truth is, the Internet plays a really big role in your every-day life—all day long. Think about it:

7:00

Your mom looks up today's weather online. "Wear your jacket. It looks like rain," she says.

8:30

At school, you hop on the library computer to do research for a report on clown fish. You type "clown fish facts" in the search engine and discover that clown fish are only a few inches long. You find lots of photos to print out for your report, too.

12:00

You're craving pizza because you checked the school Web site last night and saw pizza on today's menu. You buy a slice, plus a salad, a cookie, and milk. "Your lunch account is getting low," says the lunch lady as she checks your balance. "Remind your mom to put some more money in there by tomorrow."

1:00

Thunder booms outside your science classroom. "Here's a great Web site about weather," says your teacher. "Check out these cool weather games that teach you about different kinds of storm clouds."

4:00

A rainy afternoon is perfect for playing games on your favorite virtual-pet game site. "Meet me online," you tell your friends as you hop off the school bus.

6:00

After dinner, you notice your older brother is downloading tunes from his online music collection. "Check out this new band," he says, holding the headphone to your ear.

7:00

You send an e-mail to Grandma. "Hey, Grandma. How's the weather? It's pouring rain today." She replies right away, "It's sunny here. How's the science fair project going? Miss you. ;)"

7:30

You surf the Net for science fair project ideas and find two good ones. You print out the topics to show to your teacher tomorrow.

8:00

Mom's paying bills online, and it reminds you about lunch. "I need more lunch money in my account," you tell her. With the click of a button, Mom transfers enough money for another week of pizza, subs, and salads— and a few cookies, too.

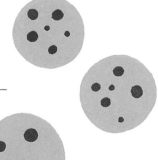

girls' favorite things

Learning, talking, playing, and planning—these are just a few of the things girls like you use the Internet for every day. And as you get older, there will be even more opportunities to use the Internet to make things happen.

Millions of girls are online right now. What do they like to do?

"Some of my favorite things to do on the Internet are playing games, listening to music, and e-mailing my friends. I also enjoy buying online treats for my Web pets."

"I like to e-mail my friends to keep up with what's new in their lives, especially during summer vacation."

"I like playing solitaire."

"I love to go on different Web sites and explore. I can make characters and earn prizes by playing games."

"I send e-cards to friends when it's their birthday or if they have a bad day."

"I use the Internet to research things for school projects. This summer I even helped Mom research what to do during our vacation."

"I like to look up the bands that play my favorite music. I love listening to new music and downloading songs."

"I use the Internet to translate words from other languages and find quizzes that help me study for tests."

"If I am having trouble with homework, I look it up on the Internet. I had to do a map of Africa, but I forgot my book at school. I looked up Africa online and filled in the map without having to go back to school."

are you ready to connect?

Riding your bike to school requires maturity, awareness, and confidence. So does babysitting or walking to the ice cream store with friends. And so does being online. Going online may not seem like a big deal, but it's a huge responsibility. There are important things to understand about the Internet before you start exploring.

Are you ready to connect? Let's find out. Decide whether each of these sentences is true or false, and circle your answers:

1. The Internet connects me to the whole wide world.

True   **False**

2. I'm safe if I connect to the Internet on my own home computer.

True   **False**

3. If I don't want to connect to something inappropriate, I can just avoid it.

True   **False**

4. Blocking all the bad sites will make the computer safe.

True   **False**

5. Parents don't know much about the Internet.

True   **False**

Answers

1. True. The most important thing to understand about the Internet is that it connects you to people and places far beyond your school friends and favorite game sites. Millions of people are online every day, around the clock.

2. False. When you're sitting online at home, it feels safe, secure, and quiet. Your home computer may even have some extra safety software installed. **But it's not just software that keeps you safe online**—it's smarts. Whether you're at school, home, or a friend's house, understanding how the Internet works will help you make smart choices and stay safe.

3. False. There are some ways that **you can accidentally connect with people and view information that you don't want to**—even if you're being careful. That's why it's important for adults to know where you're going and where you've been online.

4. False. Blocking sites that are not appropriate for kids can help make your home or school computer safer. But **there are hundreds of new sites registered every day.** Some of these sites are great tools that help kids learn and have fun. Others are not. The bottom line is that it's impossible to block every inappropriate site out there, which is why girls need to be on their guard.

5. False—and O.K., maybe a little bit true. Some parents know a lot, and others just a little. One thing parents do know is that they want their kids to be safe. And parents have a lot of experience when it comes to friends, strangers, and exploring new territory. They may not have grown up with a computer in the house, but they have life experience that can help you as you explore the Internet. And **they're counting on you to show them what you know,** too.

How'd you do? If you answered all the questions right, you're off to a good start. And if you missed a few, don't worry. We've got lots of information that will help you get plugged in.

safety first

Staying safe online is a lot like staying safe offline. For instance:

When you ride your bike, you wear a helmet and follow the rules of the road.

When you're online, you follow the rules your parents and school set for you.

When you begin to stay home by yourself, you don't answer the door when a stranger knocks.

Online, you don't answer messages from strangers, either.

When you go swimming, you stay away from the deep end of the pool until your swimming skills get stronger.

Online, you connect to Web sites that are created for kids, where you can build your online skills.

Rules change from family to family and from place to place.
See for yourself.

At home

Not allowed on the computer when your parents aren't home?
Do they monitor your e-mail and block Web sites they think
are harmful? Whatever your family rules are, following them will
help you earn respect from your parents—and more freedom and
responsibility down the road. If you have friends over, make sure
they follow your family rules, too. Their behavior will ultimately
be your responsibility.

At school

Schools have to take extra precautions to make sure kids are safe,
so you might only be able to go to certain Web sites. It might be
tempting to surf the Internet or play a quick game while you're
waiting for help, but don't do it. Your teacher is counting on you
to stick to the lesson plan and be responsible online.

At the public library

At the library, kids use computers for schoolwork and to play games.
The library lets you go almost anywhere online if you have a library
card. Most school libraries have programs on the computers that
block inappropriate sites. But many public libraries don't use filters
or blocks, so you'll need to be extra careful.

At a friend's house

Does your friend have a computer in her room? Is she allowed
to play games all night? Every family has different rules for
computer use. You should log on only when your friend's parents
are home, and make sure to ask permission. Respect her family's
rules, but stick to your own when making choices about what's
O.K. and not O.K. for *you* to do online.

how private are you?

Being private on the Internet is an important part of staying safe. And how private you are in everyday life says a lot about how private you tend to be online. Circle the answer that sounds like you.

1. You get an A on your math test.

   a. You tell the whole class.

   b. You tell your parents.

2. You have a fight with your best friend.

   a. You tell everyone on the bus about your argument.

   b. You tell your mom, who reminds you that even friends have disagreements once in a while.

3. You meet up with friends at the roller rink. You strike up a conversation with a new girl who wants to meet you all at the skating rink next week.

   a. You give her your e-mail address and tell her to e-mail you.

   b. You tell her you'll give her a call if you plan on skating next week.

4. You have the stomach flu and miss a few days of school. When you return, friends ask how you're feeling.

   a. You give them the gory details of your illness, including your temperature and number of trips to the bathroom.

   b. You say, "Much better," and leave it at that.

5. Your grandmother gave you $50 for your birthday to buy a new jean jacket. Your friends ask you where you got it.

   a. You tell your friends it cost $50 and you got it at a fancy store at the mall.

   b. You tell your friends it was a gift from your grandmother.

Answers

Jaw flapper
If you answered **a** to every question, you're a pretty outgoing person. And sometimes, you share more information than you ought to. You'll have to practice hard to stay private.

Loose lips
If you answered both **a**'s and **b**'s, you are private about some subjects but not others. Give yourself more time to think before you share information. When in doubt, keep it to yourself.

Lips zipped
A score of all **b**'s means you're pretty private. You tend to keep things to yourself or just within your immediate circle. This is a very good trait to have when you're connecting online.

Why is privacy so important online?

Because the Internet is a public place. It doesn't feel that way when you're typing away alone at home or at school. **But anything you say or do online can potentially be seen by your whole school, your whole town—even the whole world—with just the click of a mouse.** Friends can forward an e-mail to everyone they know— even accidentally. Or someone can print out an e-mail and pass it around the school. Or someone might copy your e-mail and post it online. That's why it's really important to practice being private when you use the Internet.

that's personal

Here's a list of things that you should *never* share online:

Name, age, and birthday
As a general rule, don't give out anything with a number in it. Most of that will be private information. And never, ever share your full name online.

E-mail address and phone number
Your contact information should be shared only with your close friends and family, and any passwords or log-on codes are for your eyes only.

What you look like
Your friends already know you have blonde hair or brown eyes. They know whether you're tall or have dark skin. Keeping your appearance private is important when you're online.

Where you can be found
Never give out your location, such as your home address or the name of your school, online.

Family facts
Whether your parents are married, how much your mom's car costs, and what your grades are—these are all personal. Even if this information doesn't identify you, it's personal and should remain private.

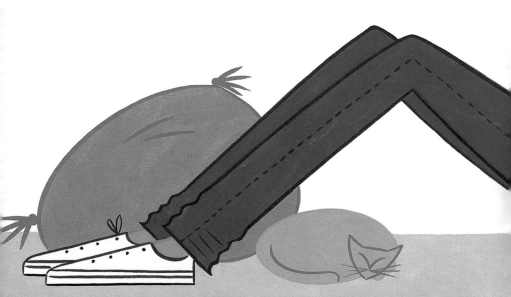

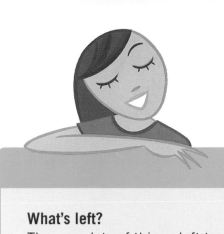

What's left?
There are lots of things left to share: how much you love the latest band, what you thought about the new summer movie in theaters, and how excited you are for summer vacation. Sharing information without lots of personal details can seem strange at first, but with practice, you'll find there really is a lot left to say.

what do you do?

The more time you spend on the Internet, the more you may "meet" other people who want to connect with you. But just as in real life, you should never talk with strangers. Sure, it's O.K. to connect with classmates or friends from summer camp. But what about your friend's cousin? Or your friend's friend's cousin?

Decide which of these connections sound safe to you. Would you respond?

Hi! ;) This is Maya's sister Ruby. How R U? Maya gave me your e-mail. Please write back.

Your good friend Maya told you her little sister just got an e-mail address. She asked if Ruby could send you an e-mail. Since you were expecting her message, it's probably O.K. to respond. If you're not sure, call Maya to check that the message you got was from Ruby.

Hey there! What are you doing tonight? Wanna meet at the park? See you at 5:00. JAJ

You have a friend named J.J. and another named Julie Jones, but you don't recognize the e-mail address. Don't respond. Whenever you're going to connect with friends, call first to make sure they actually did send the e-mail. And never, ever meet up with someone you don't already know.

Hey, who is this? I got your e-mail from Jennifer's list. If u r kewl, mail me back. Joe S.

Right away it's easy to tell you don't know this person—and he doesn't know you. If your e-mail gets forwarded around, you may get random e-mails from people you don't know who just want to start a conversation. Even if this guy sounds harmless online, you don't know a thing about him. That means he's a stranger—so hit the delete button.

What's up? I'm having a sleepover Saturday and you're invited. Hope you can make it! Ava

Your friend Ava is always making last-minute plans, but there are a few red flags in this e-mail. First, it didn't come from her regular e-mail address. She didn't use your name, and there are no other details about the sleepover—a time or location. Sometimes kids at school or older siblings will pull pranks over e-mail. Make sure it's not a prank by calling Ava to see what's really up for the weekend.

The rule when connecting online is to **place the face.** In other words, unless you already know a person from school or soccer or Scouts, that person is a stranger.

connecting offline

Hanging out offline with friends you know is great. But agreeing to make a real-life connection with someone you met online is NEVER a good idea. Why? Because just as in the real world, there are folks online with bad intentions who may try to connect with kids. They may use tricks to get kids interested.

Some might promise you a prize:
Meet me, and I'll give you tickets to the JoJo Brothers Band concert.

Some might use compliments:
We saw your picture and think you have modeling potential. Come to the food court at the mall tomorrow at noon for an interview.

Some might try to convince you that you already know them:
I'm new at your school and haven't made many friends. You seem pretty nice. Can you meet me at the bus stop tomorrow and show me around?

Some may act as if they already know you:
I know your family from the neighborhood and wondered if you'd like one of my new puppies. Can you stop by after school tomorrow?

Better safe than sorry. NEVER meet someone in person who contacts you through the Internet. If you're unsure, talk to your parents about the situation. Even when you are making plans with friends you know, always let a grown-up in on your plans.

savvy surfing

You've probably spent time on the Internet looking for information for a book report or a science project. Maybe a friend told you about a funny Web site, and you've searched around to find it. Or you saw a TV show that had a Web site and decided to visit.

There is a lot of information on the Internet. In fact, almost anything you can think of is on there—the good and the bad. That's why it's important to learn some tips for staying safe and finding what you need.

Use a protected computer.
School computers are often set up to block Web sites that are not appropriate for kids. Those filters also make finding what you want much easier.

Search first.
Before you type a Web site into the address bar at the top of the page, do it in a search engine. That way, even if you've spelled the Web address wrong, there's a good chance the search engine will find the site you want to visit.

Ask friends.
If you're working on a school project, ask your teacher for recommendations on which sites have the best information. If you're looking for a great Web site on a popular movie star, ask the kids at the lunch table. Finding out about great sites from friends and teachers will cut your surfing time in half.

Use a "favorites" list.

If you go to certain sites often—for homework help, to play games, or to check on your favorite sports team—save them in your computer's "favorites" folder. This way, you won't have to search around. Your list of favorites will always be ready for you to click.

Write down the site.

When you discover a great Web site, write it down. That way, you can take it with you to school or to a friend's house, and you won't have to surf all over trying to find it again. Keep track of your favorite sites on the journal pages at the back of this book.

Yikes! When you were searching for a Web site on adopting a new kitten, something really creepy and gross popped up. Now you can't get it off the computer. What do you do?

First of all, don't panic. Most girls have stumbled upon a Web site with disturbing photos or content at least once. Close the Web site right away if you can, and let your parents know what happened. Worried that your parents will think you visited the site on purpose? Don't be. If you go to your parents right away, you're showing them how responsible and trustworthy you are. They can block the site and make sure that you—and the computer—are protected.

P.O.S.
(parent over shoulder)

Parents. They're always wondering what you're doing—especially when you're on the Internet. If your parents hover over you while you're online, don't be surprised. They were there as you took your first steps. They stood by you as you learned to ride a bike. Connecting online is like surfing the world, so you can bet they want to watch out for you online, too.

Parents play a really important part in your Internet life, for three reasons:

1. They pay for the computer you use and the Internet connection.

2. There's a good chance they've spent time installing programs on your home computer and created rules to keep you safe.

3. They care about you. If you run into anything upsetting or confusing, they are there to help you out.

Remember: Your parents probably didn't grow up using the Internet, so some of this is new to them, too. But they have loads of life experience that helps them identify a bad situation or deal with something creepy. You can help them—and yourself—by showing them what you like to do, sharing what you've discovered online, and letting them know when something weird is going on.

Even when your parents aren't watching over your shoulder, they may be using tools to protect you. Here are a few:

Security software. This helps protect the computer from *viruses*— programs that can harm your computer, destroy your files, and put your whole computer system on the fritz. Some security software also allows parents to block Web sites that are not for kids.

Filters. Just as the word suggests, these programs can be used to filter out bad words or Web sites with a bad reputation.

Monitors. These allow your parents to keep track of your behavior online. Your parents may want to see copies of your e-mail conversations to make sure your friends are acting appropriately. Or they may keep track of which sites you visit online. Monitors let your parents supervise you from a distance, just as they did when you first started riding a bike. You won't really see them there, but you'll know they've got their eyes on you.

Don't they trust me?
They sure want to. And once you show them that you are a responsible Internet user, they will probably spend less time checking up on you. But you've got to earn their confidence.

So instead of rolling your eyes when Mom checks in, let her know you understand how important security and safety are when it comes to the Internet.

it's a deal

Earn some points with Mom and Dad by following the rules they set for going online. Not sure what the rules are? Talk to your parents.

Prepare for the talk by making a list of your favorite things to do online (such as playing games, e-mailing your friends, or looking up your favorite band). Also list what you *want* to do (such as join a new game site, download music, make movies, or get an IM account). To keep the conversation rolling and make sure the whole family agrees, talk through the questions on page 29. Or visit "Fun for Girls" at americangirl.com for a printable questionnaire and other activities from *A Smart Girl's Guide to the Internet.*

May I go online when you aren't home? ☐ yes ☐ no

Is there any computer in the house that is off-limits to me?

_____

Are there certain sites I'm not allowed to go on?

_____

Is there a limit to how much time I can spend online?

_____

May my friends use our home computer? ☐ yes ☐ no

Are there certain programs I'm not allowed to use?

_____

What are the consequences for breaking the house rules?

_____

Another question I have is

_____

_____?

Another way to build trust is with an Internet contract, a promise to your parents that you will act responsibly online. Visit "Fun for Girls" at americangirl.com to design your own contract and to find other activities from *A Smart Girl's Guide to the Internet*.

Top Ten Rules for Staying Safe Online

1. I will not give out personal information, such as my address and telephone number, online.

2. I will tell a parent right away if I come across anything online that makes me feel uncomfortable or scared.

3. I will never agree to get together with someone I "met" online unless a parent goes with me.

4. I will check with a parent before sending someone my photo online.

5. I will not send hurtful messages online, and if I receive one, I won't respond. Instead, I'll tell a parent right away.

6. I will not give out my Internet passwords to anyone other than my parents.

7. I will check with a parent before downloading software.

8. I will ask a parent before I sign up or register for any accounts online.

9. I will respect my parents' house rules for the Internet.

10. I'll share with my parents some of my favorite things to do online so that we can have fun together.

I promise to follow these rules to stay safe and have fun online.

Girl's signature_____

_____Date_____

I will protect my daughter by making sure these rules are followed. If something happens online that makes her feel scared or uncomfortable, I will do my best to help her work through it.

Parent's signature_____

_____Date_____

express
yourself

let's talk tech

Your favorite TV star has an e-mail address. Your teacher sends e-mails to your parents. Kids in school may be exchanging instant-message screen names, and you've heard of others who have visited chat rooms. It seems as if everybody is talking online. And you want to get in on the conversation, right?

Expressing yourself online can be a blast. Maybe you have your own e-mail address or have wanted to try instant messaging with a friend. Maybe you're trying to convince your parents to let you visit a chat room.

Whether you're already connecting with friends and family through the Internet or just getting started, reviewing the do's and don'ts of what to say online is important. And understanding the difference between e-mail, instant messaging, and chat rooms will help you figure out what type of expression is right for you right now.

e-mail do's and don'ts

More than a billion people in the world use e-mail, and hundreds of billions of e-mail messages are sent every day. That's millions of e-mails per second—a lot more mail than your mail carrier could lug through your neighborhood, that's for sure.

Typing a quick e-mail to a friend may seem like a no-brainer, but you do need to use your brain when you have an e-mail address of your own. Follow these tips to keep your e-mail box free from junk mail, bullies, and cyber bugs:

Think public.
Think of e-mail as a postcard—a message without an envelope. Your e-mail makes a few stops as it travels through cyberspace, and it could be seen by someone other than the friend you sent it to. Once it arrives in your friend's e-mail box, it could be seen by a little brother peeking over your friend's shoulder. Or it could be printed out and posted in the school cafeteria, or accidentally forwarded to everyone in your friend's e-mail address book.

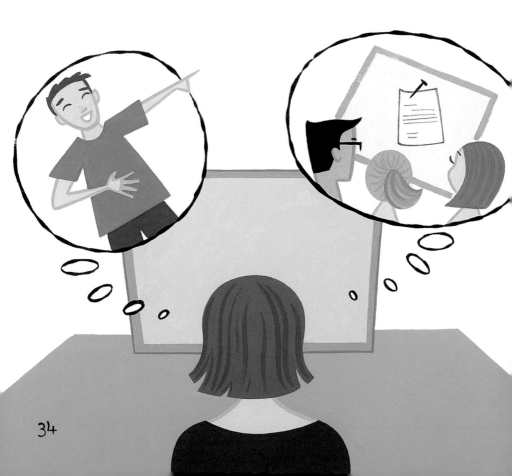

Keep your e-mail address private.
You wouldn't give your phone number to a stranger, so don't give out your e-mail address when filling out a survey or shopping at the mall.

Keep friends' e-mail addresses private, too.
Don't give out or forward an e-mail address without the permission of the owner.

Never open an e-mail from someone you don't know.
If you receive an e-mail from someone you haven't given your e-mail address to, don't open the message.

Beware of links.
If your friend e-mails you a link to a fun game or Web site, think twice before you click on the link. Some links can lead you to sites that record your address and will send you spam. If you recognize the link, go for it. If not, ask your parents before you click.

Be careful about opening attachments.
Sometimes friends will attach funny pictures or jokes, but these can contain computer viruses—dangerous programs that can harm your computer. Always ask a parent before opening an attachment.

What is spam?
Three out of four e-mails that are sent every day are *spam*. Spam is like the junk mail you get in your real mailbox. It might be an advertisement trying to sell you something, or it might be a message delivering a *virus,* a program that can mess up your computer. Spam can fill up your inbox with unwanted—even dangerous—e-mail messages. That's one reason you need to really *think* before you open messages and attachments.

instant messaging

Instant messaging, often called IM for short, is almost like talking on the phone—except it's typing through the computer. You type something and press "send," and it arrives on your friend's screen, well, in an instant.

Just like e-mail, IM is a fun way to connect with your buddies. In fact, when you use IM, you create a *buddy list,* names of your friends who also have IM. What should you know about IM? Read the tips below to find out.

Watch out for viruses.
Just as with e-mail, you can get a computer virus through an IM message. That's why you need to know your buddies and stick to your buddy list. Ask your parents if your computer has security software to protect against viruses. And always check with a parent before opening links or attachments.

Don't share too much.
Most IM programs allow you to add cool pictures to your buddy icon to give it a personal touch. Some also allow you to add personal information. But personal information is private, so keep it to yourself. Don't use personal information when creating your online screen name, and never give out your phone number or address during an IM conversation. If you attach clip art or a cute cartoon to your online account, choose something that doesn't give away any personal information.

Know your buddies.
Your friends, your cousins, or even a sibling will probably be on your buddy list. Your buddies may want to connect you to other people they know, too. For instance, your friend may want you to add her neighbor to your list. Or your cousin may want you to add her study partner as a buddy. But you wouldn't talk to strangers in real life, and unless you're introduced in person first, don't use IM to talk to buddies you don't know.

hannah

emma

tyler

jessica

ryan

dress it up

When you write a message by hand, you can add lots of personal touches to make it your own. When you e-mail or instant message, you can be creative, too. Here's how:

Add color.
Use colored type to express your mood or your personality. An e-mail about your new favorite song might be pink with excitement. A message about your Halloween costume might be orange and black. Add lots of different colors for a rainbow effect.

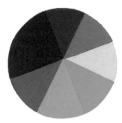

Add style.
Use **bold** or *italic* type for words you want to draw attention to. You can even change the size of your type. It can be really fun to mix type sizes and styles!

Add a background.
Some e-mail programs let you put cool background pictures in your messages, such as pretty flowers or a beach scene. See if your e-mail has background settings.

Add emoticons.

Emoticons are symbols that help you express emotion online, whether you're feeling happy, sad, or silly. Try some of these:

:)	happy	<3	sideways heart, or "love"
;)	wink, or "just kidding"	;D	laughing
:(	sad	:'(	crying
:0)	smiley with a nose	:$	embarrassed
>:(	angry	:\	undecided
:P	sticking out your tongue	:!	foot in mouth
8)	cool	:0	surprised

do u know net lingo?

Net lingo uses letters and numbers to stand for words and sentences. Lots of kids use this code when they e-mail or IM. Net lingo is fun and can save you time—but only if you *really* know what you are talking about. Do you know what each of these sayings means?

1. *LOL*
a. Lots of love
b. Laugh out loud
c. Lick of lemon

2. *iDK*
a. I don't know.
b. I dig kittens.
c. Impressive designer knits

3. *BFF*
a. Big furry feet
b. Best friends forever
c. Born free forever

4. *OMG*
a. On my guard
b. Only my girlfriends
c. Oh my goodness

5. *RTFL*
a. Rotten or totally foul language
b. Rolling on the floor laughing
c. Running out for lunch

6. *ASL*
a. Ask someone later
b. Age, sex, location
c. All summer long

Answers

1. Both **a** and **b** are right, depending on the context.

2. **a**

3. **b**

4. **c**

5 **b**

6. **b**—and this one is a red flag. Never give any of this information out. It's all private, and anyone asking you is a stranger.

Beware
Sometimes girls use codes like these to say swear words or other things they wouldn't say in person. If you get net lingo you don't understand, ask your friend to spell it out. If she won't tell you the meaning, just log off. And never use abbreviations that *you* don't know the meaning of, either.

what do you do?

Because net lingo and emoticons can be hard to interpret, there's a lot of room for misunderstanding online. And girls can get carried away when pouring out their feelings in an e-mail or IM. That's why it's always best to have important conversations face-to-face.

Mad at a friend because she didn't invite you to her birthday party?

Think twice before you write your angry IM or e-mail. Angry messages sent in the heat of the moment are called *flames* and can cause you big trouble. Before you sit down at the computer in a fit of rage, sit down with a pencil and write out your feelings. If you're still angry the next day, call your friend or arrange a face-to-face meeting. That way, when you find your invitation stuck in the back of the mailbox, there will be no hard feelings.

Just joking around?

Jokes don't always come across as funny online. Let's say you sent your friend an e-mail saying, "Skating was a blast, but you need more practice." Face-to-face, you'd smile, and she could see by your expression that you were just kidding. After all, she fell only twice, and *you* spent most of your time on the floor! But over the Internet, your friend may misunderstand. She may think you're saying that her skating skills stink. Before you say something silly online, think about how your words might come across. To play it safe, save your jokes for when you're together.

Upset to hear that your friend's grandma died?

An e-mail expressing your condolences is a nice thought, but your friend needs a hug. When bad things happen, it can be uncomfortable to face your friends and it might seem easier to send an e-mail. But an e-mail can never replace the presence of a good friend, and just being there during tough times shows you care.

Excited about plans you're making?

Maybe you're planning a sleepover or an end-of-the-summer party. It's easy to whip off an e-mail to all your friends telling them about the party, but remember that plans may change. What if your mom decides you can invite only one or two friends? Always talk to your parents and firm up plans before you share them online. If you want to bounce ideas off someone, talk with a friend face-to-face, and ask her to keep the conversation to herself until you work out all the details.

Embarrassed by something that happened in gym class?

Let's say that while you were doing jumping jacks, you accidentally hit a classmate in the face—and she went to the nurse's office for an ice pack. You e-mail a friend saying, "You'll never believe what happened in gym class. I smacked Bella in the face!" Without the details, your friend might wonder if you hit Bella on purpose or whether Bella is O.K. Your friend might even forward the e-mail on to others who take it the wrong way. To save yourself from extra embarrassment, share stories like this one in person. That way your friends can ask questions, and you can explain what *really* happened.

chat rooms

Chat rooms are places where people can go online to talk about a certain subject, such as soccer or stray dogs. Chat rooms are usually filled with strangers who come together to share stories, advice, or ideas about something they have in common. The key word here is "strangers." No matter how interested you are in soccer or stray dogs, sharing your stories with strangers is never a good idea.

Are all chat rooms off-limits?
There are a few exceptions to the rule—certain chat rooms are designed just for kids. These are usually monitored to make sure no one is saying things that are inappropriate. Other Web sites allow families to set up their own private chat rooms so that only your brothers, cousins, or grandma can join the chat.

Before you join a chat room—even one that claims to be created for girls—have a face-to-face chat with your parents. It's the best way to be safe and a great sign that you're really beginning to understand this Internet stuff. Your parents will be proud.

45

blogs

The word *blog* comes from two words—*Web*, meaning the World Wide Web, and *log*, as in journal or diary. Jotting down your thoughts and opinions on a Web page has become a way for people to share their ideas. There are blogs about all sorts of things, from endangered whales and the environment to marathons, movies, and fashion.

Some blogging programs require kids to be 13 or older in order to have a blog. But there are other great ways to explore the world of blogs.

Read blogs.
Ask your parents or your teacher to help you find some blogs written by kids. Reading them will help you get a feel for how blogs look and sound. If you're interested in posting a response, ask your parents for permission.

Start a family blog.
Talk to your parents about setting up a family blog, maybe centered around a special event or a summer trip. Each member of your family can take turns writing memories along the way. Some blogs are set up so that only the close friends and family members you choose can visit your blog.

Keep a computer diary.
Until you can have a blog of your own, try keeping a diary on the computer using a word-processing program. Log in each day, put the date on the page, and record your thoughts. When you're ready to start a new week or month, print out your diary so that you have a printed copy.

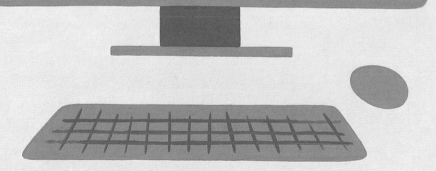

The Smith Family Blog

Posted by Chloe on 11/16 7:46 a.m.
Sammy woke me up REALLY early this morning. I could hear him meowing from the kitchen. Everyone else was sleeping, but Sammy and I got up to play – just the two of us. He likes his toy mouse, but he likes my shoelaces even more.

Mom on 11/15 7:32 p.m.
Here's a photo of the newest member of our family: Sam. As you can tell, he's already made himself at home!

Posted by Chloe on 11/14 8:10 p.m.
We picked out our kitty today! As soon as I saw Sammy, I knew he was the one. I think he knew it too. When I picked him up, he nibbled on my finger and gave me a kitty kiss. His tongue tickled my hand. I love him already!

social networks

What's a social network? Believe it or not, you already have one in real life. A *social network* is the circle of friends and acquaintances you interact with every day.

There are also social networks online. Usually these sites let you build your own Web page, express yourself, and connect with a bunch of friends and acquaintances. Do you want to connect with friends through an online social network? Of course you do. And as you can see, you already are. You're e-mailing friends. You're playing games on sites where you can connect with your friends. Maybe you're about to try instant messaging. These are all great practice for being part of a bigger online social network someday.

Why can't I join now?

Most of the large social networks are designed for folks 13 or older—sometimes *way* older. The language, conversations, and subject matter are really geared toward an older crowd.

Besides, most of your friends aren't there yet, and you should never connect with strangers. So be patient, smart, and safe. Social networks will be around for a long time, and when you and your friends are ready and you have your parents' permission, you can give one a try. Until then, the best way to prove you're ready is to practice privacy and be responsible in whatever you do online.

Your friend just joined a popular social network, where she can post a profile of herself and her interests. She's only 11, but she lied about her age and wants you to sign up, too.
Hold on. Hopefully you see a few warning signs here. First, your friend lied—never a good way to demonstrate responsible online behavior. Second, she may have broken the rules of the site. Most social networks require members to be at least 13. And finally, she's trying to coax you to break the rules and lie, too. Your answer? Tell her no way. Although it can be tempting to try, you'll be putting your own reputation on the line. And if you break the rules now, your parents may have a hard time trusting you later—when you *are* old enough to sign up.

smart girls know this

Whether you're sending e-mail or instant messages, playing a game online, or visiting a parent-approved chat room, there are three main things to remember:

1. **Place the face.** Make sure you are e-mailing, instant messaging, or connecting only with those people you know well in real life. If a friend offers to pass along the e-mail or screen name for her brother, cousin, or friend, say no.

2. **Stay private.** Be careful about what kind of information you share over the Internet. Even when you're talking to friends or relatives, you never know who is in the room with them or who might have access to your friend's inbox. And never give out someone else's private information, including e-mail address or screen name.

3. **Sign up with a parent.** It's really important that parents know who you're talking to and what you're doing online. That way, if anything strange or unusual happens or if there are hidden costs involved, parents can help you work things out. Before you sign up for an online account of any kind, ask your mom or dad for permission.

cyber-bullying

bullies online

There are all different kinds of bullies. At school, there are bullies who say mean things to you. Some may gossip or spread rumors about you to others. Some may exclude you from clubs or games. Other bullies might actually threaten to hurt you on the playground, take your lunch, or push you out of their way in the hall.

There are also bullies online. We call them *cyberbullies* because they use the tools on the Internet—sometimes called *cyberspace*—to hurt others. Cyberbullies are different from school bullies in a few ways. They can bully around the clock, e-mailing and instant messaging all night long. They can spread bad things about you in a very short time, with the click of a mouse. And they hide behind computers, which means they're often anonymous. You can't see their faces or hear their voices—you can only see their e-mail addresses or screen names. But one thing's for sure—they *are* bullies. And bullying behavior, whether on the playground or online, is **never** O.K.

A cyberbully might . . .

make you feel left out of an online game or block you from her buddy list.
You can't be in our group. We already have enough players.

send e-mails saying cruel things.
Your hair is ugly.

use angry or rude language.
WE DON'T LIKE YOU!

share embarrassing information or photos of you with others.
She wears hand-me-down clothes. You can see them in this photo.

send threats to scare you.
If you ride the bus, I'm going to hurt you.

you're not alone

Have you ever received an e-mail or instant message that scared you or hurt your feelings? Many girls have. In fact, cyberbullying is a big problem for today's girls. See what other girls have to say about bullies online.

"Someone I know from school sent me an e-mail that said I look ugly in my new glasses."

"One of my friends slipped and got hurt badly at school. When she got home from the doctor, she got e-mails calling her 'klutzy' because she slipped."

"People send nasty messages to other people because they think it's fun. I think it's wrong because it hurts people's feelings."

"Cyberbullying makes you feel like you're being watched, because you don't always know who's doing it."

"The worst part about cyberbullying is that the whole school can all of a sudden know stuff about you, even if it's not true."

"Someone at school got a mean e-mail that my friend supposedly sent. The person got mad and started yelling at my friend. She started to cry, because the e-mail wasn't from her."

what would you do?

How would you handle each of these cyberbullying scenarios?

When you log into your IM after school, you find out Bailey has blocked you from her IM buddy list. You try to connect with Kelsey, only to discover you've been blocked from her list, too. Same thing happens with Mia. When you approach the girls at school, they give you the cold shoulder. What did you do wrong? Chances are, you did nothing wrong. But being suddenly blocked from your buddies' lists without warning or explanation can make you feel left out, rotten, and downright bullied. Friends who gang up and exclude you from online conversation without reason aren't friends. Log off—and reconnect with friends you can count on.

You're excited to see you have six new messages in your inbox from Jenna, a popular girl at school. Every message, however, says something mean about you. What do you do? Saying something mean online is sneaky, cowardly, and, worst of all, hurtful. Mean or rude language can also get girls into big trouble with parents, the school, and sometimes even the police. If you get a mean message, talk to an adult you trust right away, such as a parent, a teacher, or a guidance counselor. Whatever you do, don't respond to the message. Lashing back will just fuel the bully's fire.

During a sleepover at your house, your friends decide to send an e-mail to Sarah, who couldn't come. They want to tell her what a good time they are having without her. You don't want to do it, but everyone else seems to think it's a funny idea. Trust your instincts. Jokes and sarcastic remarks don't always come through clearly online. Even if you don't mean to bully Sarah, this e-mail may hurt her feelings and make her feel even more left out than she does already. Speak up, and try to help your friends see the difference between a funny joke and a hurtful prank. Ask a parent to step in if you need to.

how to stand strong

Treat cyberbullying the same way you would treat bullying in the hallways at school or at the bus stop. Follow these steps to stop a bully in his or her tracks:

1. **Don't react.** It might be tempting to "punch back" at a cyber-bully, but responding gives bullies exactly what they want— a reaction. Never respond to a mean or threatening message.

2. **Record what happened.** You can print out an e-mail as proof of what is going on. It's often easier to show someone a hard copy, especially if you need to share it with a school official. Whatever you do, don't erase a mean message until after you've shown it to a grown-up.

3. **Tell an adult.** Resist the urge to tell your friends or forward the bullying message to others. That just creates more drama and gives the bully more power. Instead, tell an adult you trust so that he or she can help you think through your options.

Who can you tell? There are lots of people who can help.

Your family
They may not all know as much as you do about computers, but parents, grandparents, and older brothers and sisters *do* know about bullies. They can help you work through bad feelings and put a stop to the bullying.

Your teacher
If cyberbullying happens when you are online at school, tell your teacher right away. Your teacher will want to keep an eye on the situation. Even if bullying isn't happening on school grounds, it affects your feelings at school. It may help you to let your teacher know what's going on.

Guidance counselors
These folks have had plenty of experience with bullying in school, on the playground, and online. Talk to your guidance counselor. Chances are, you aren't the only one being bullied. You may help other students by letting your guidance counselor know what's happening with you.

Isn't it tattling when you tell an adult?
Nope. When you tattle, you're trying to make someone look bad. But when you tell an adult about bullying, you're trying to stop someone from hurting you or someone else. Asking for help is the best way to get the situation resolved and to keep the Internet safe— for you *and* for others.

check yourself

It's easier than you think to take part in cyberbullying behavior. Have *you* ever said something mean over the Internet? Or played a not-so-funny prank on someone online? Before you send an e-mail or instant message, do a quick check:

☐ **Read your message out loud.**
Is it clear? Is it kind? Reading your message out loud helps you hear how it might sound if you said it to someone face-to-face.

☐ **Picture your friend's reaction.**
How do you think your friend will feel when she reads the message? If the answer is confused, sad, worried, or angry, don't send the message.

☐ **Count to ten.**
This gives you one more chance to read your message—and to rewrite it if you need to.

photos, videos & music

digital photos

Digital cameras and camera phones make it easy to take oodles of photos, and sharing those photos is nearly as much fun as taking them. E-mailing photos to friends or loading them onto a family Web site is a great way to give people a peek into your life. But do you know when it's O.K. to share photos—and when it's O.K. even to take them in the first place? Take this quiz to find out.

to share or not to share?

Would you share these photos with friends? Circle your answers.

1. You snuck into your sister's room and got a close-up of her sleeping—with her mouth open.

share   delete

2. You caught an "action shot" of your friend Ashley slipping and falling at the ice rink.

share   delete

3. You're away at camp, and you snap a shot of the amazing sunset.

share   delete

4. Your dad got a great shot of your softball team celebrating after your big win.

share   delete

Answers

1. Delete it. The photo may be funny, but taking it was taking advantage. You didn't have your sister's permission to take the shot, which means you don't have her permission to *share* it, either.

2. Delete it, especially if your friend was embarrassed or hurt by the fall. Was she O.K. afterward? Did the two of you laugh about it? If so, you can share the shot with her, but don't share it with anyone else without her permission.

3. Share it. Scenery shots are usually O.K. to share, and they're a great way to say to family and friends, "I wish you were here, too!"

4. Share the picture, but only with your teammates. When people are posing and smiling, you've usually got the green light to snap a photo. And they'll usually be glad to have a copy for themselves.

Get the picture? Always stop to think before you e-mail a photo to your whole address book. Just because you *can* take a picture and share it online doesn't mean you should. Here are a few more photo do's and don'ts:

Do e-mail photos to your parents, grandparents, cousins, and best friends.

Don't e-mail photos to people you don't know well or haven't met face-to-face.

Do ask permission before you take a photo of someone.

Don't take photos of someone who doesn't know you're taking them.

Do ask for permission from parents before posting photos on a family Web site.

Don't post a photo with identifying information in it, such as a school sweatshirt, a license plate, or a street sign near your home.

Do use your pictures as a screen saver on your home computer.

Don't use your photo on an IM profile.

photos offline

Of course, you don't need to post photos online at all. There are plenty of ways to showcase your photography skills offline, too.

- Make a photo album for your best friend.

- Set up a slideshow of photos as your screen saver.

- Frame artsy prints for your room.

- Have a weekly photo contest with friends.

- Make a collage of photos for your school locker.

- Use photos to enhance a school project, such as a slideshow presentation or a book report.

- Print out photos and use them to decorate cards or gift bags.

- Discover fun craft papers for your computer printer. You can use photos to make magnets and even iron-on T-shirts!

- Become the official photographer at family get-togethers. Post the photos on a family Web site, or e-mail them to your family address book.

- Print out a photo of the week to hang on your bedroom door.

videos

Photos aren't the only way to capture fun moments in your life. Moviemaking madness is on the rise. Many digital cameras and even some cell phones can take short videos, and kids are using their creativity to make films for school and for fun.

You may have visited a popular video-sharing site where people can post funny video clips. Maybe you even want to post your own. But sharing videos is a lot like sharing photos. It's fun to share your movies with friends, but make sure you know what's O.K. to video-record—and what's not—before you put anything online.

are you a smart moviemaker?

Circle your answers below to find out.

1. While you're recording an extra-credit movie for history class, your friend starts hiccuping. She wants to do the scene over because she's embarrassed. You . . .

   a. tell her you'll edit it out, but you leave it in because it was funny.

   b. take it out but tell your class what happened while they're watching the movie.

   c. suggest a retake and respect her wishes. A good friend is worth more than a good laugh.

2. Friends want to make a movie and upload it to a popular video-sharing site. You . . .

   a. jump on board. This might be your ticket to stardom.

   b. wear a disguise and agree to a very small role.

   c. suggest to the group that you ask permission first and get help from a parent.

3. You and some friends video-record yourselves doing a great dance routine, and your parents say it's O.K. if you upload it to a video-sharing site. The first thing you do is . . .

   a. run to the computer and upload your clip.

   b. think up a funny title and add some film credits.

   c. call the friends you made it with and ask them to get permission from their parents, too.

4. A friend sends you a link to an online video from a sleepover you attended. The video stars you in curlers—snoring. You . . .

   a. wear dark glasses and a scarf to school so that no one will recognize you. How embarrassing!

   b. yell at your friend and tell everyone that she betrayed you.

   c. tell the moviemaker that you're embarrassed, and ask her to remove the video.

Answers

Two thumbs up

If you answered mostly c's, you know how to make movies *and* smart choices. Respecting the privacy of other people and protecting your own reputation takes courage and smarts. And keeping your parents in the loop really shows your maturity. Encore!

One thumb up, one thumb down

If you answered mostly b's, you sometimes miss your cues when it comes to making good decisions. You're definitely creative, but don't let it get in the way of privacy—or your reputation.

Two thumbs down

If you answered mostly a's, you sometimes let your enthusiasm for the dramatic get the best of you. And if you're not careful, you could really get hurt. Making fun of friends and posting videos without permission are big mistakes—mistakes that could cost you friendships and Internet privileges.

more movie fun

Having fun with videos isn't only about posting them online. Read on to discover some movie ideas for your number-one audience: yourself, your friends, and your family.

Make a video diary.
Video-record yourself talking about what's going on in your life. Sometimes it's easier to talk things out than it is to put them on paper. And you can keep your video diary private if you'd like.

Send a video message.
If you haven't seen your dad in a while, make a short video and send it to him through e-mail. You can hold up that A+ test you brought home or show off your new hairstyle.

Track your family history.
Video-record a day in the life of your family, or make a documentary at your family reunion. Interview everyone who attends, and let family members know that you'll show your movie at *next* year's reunion.

Get school credit.
For a school project or report, ask your teacher if you can make a video to share with the class. Your teacher will probably welcome your creativity, and you'll inspire your classmates, too.

Record your travels.
Make a video of your family's vacation to Mount Rushmore or the Grand Canyon. Get great footage of the best parts of the trip (look, a rainbow!) and the worst (ugh, more rain).

Host a film festival.
Make some fun short movies, and invite your family and friends to watch them. Don't forget the popcorn!

online tunes

What's the great thing about music today? You can buy it, listen to it, and even record it right on your computer. Some girls purchase songs from a Web site and download them onto an MP3 player. Other girls make CDs to play on a boom box or in the car on the way to school.

Of course, just like everything else, there are a few things to remember when you're building your music collection. Some music contains lyrics that aren't appropriate for you. And copying music isn't allowed. In fact, downloading and trading music can be illegal.

Every time someone copies a song, the singers, musicians, record company, and music stores—all the people who work to make that music available to you—lose a little money. And if everyone made copies instead of purchasing music, people in the music business would be out of business altogether.

O.K. to copy?

Take this quiz to see how savvy you are when it comes to copying music.

1. You can e-mail a copy of a popular song to a friend so that she can hear it.

True   False

2. You can copy your favorite songs, put them on a CD, and give the CD to a friend for her birthday.

True   False

3. You can burn a CD of songs you bought online so that you can listen to them in the car on your next family vacation.

True   False

4. You can lend songs to a friend to listen to.

True   False

5. You don't have to pay for free songs offered by a band promoting a new album.

True   False

Answers

1. False. When you e-mail a song, you're actually making a copy of that song. And making a copy of a song is a no-no.

2. False. Copying songs for others is almost always illegal.

3. True. If you've already purchased a song online, you can make a copy of it to listen to somewhere else. You can copy a song as long as it is for your own personal use.

4. True. Letting a friend borrow a CD to listen to songs you like is perfectly fine. That way she can find out if she likes the songs— and buy her own copies if she decides they rock.

5. True. Sometimes, you might get free songs from a band just starting out. They want to spread the news about their music, and they offer free songs for just that—sharing. If you'd like to try their music, go for it.

what do you do?

Think you've got it? Let's be sure. Read these scenarios and see if you can guess the answers.

I just downloaded a new song and want my friend to hear it. Can I attach a copy to a message I send her?
Nope. Remember, sending a song through e-mail or IM is just like stealing another copy of the song. Instead, tell your friend the name of the song and the artist. Suggest that she listen to it online to decide if she wants to buy it for her collection.

My friend just added a bunch of songs from my favorite band to her online music collection. She offered to make me a CD of the songs. Can I accept it?
Your friend is trying to be thoughtful, but you're right to think again. Thank her for her offer, but let her know that making a copy of a song—even to give to a friend—is against the law. Instead, ask if you can listen to her music the next time you're hanging out at her house.

I made a CD from my online music collection, and I want to bring the CD to a sleepover. Is that O.K.?
You bet! You can play your songs for your friends at the sleepover as long as you're not giving them copies of the music.

So . . . I can share music with friends sometimes and not others? I'm confused!
You're right—this is confusing. It's even confusing for grown-ups. The easiest rule to follow is this: If you pay, then you can play. If you purchase music online or at the store, then it is yours to enjoy. Your friends can listen to your music, but you can't send or make them a copy. If someone else purchases music, you can listen to it, but you can't add it to your collection or make a copy either.

music ratings

Movies have a rating system. Television shows and video games have rating systems. So it makes sense that music does, too.

Only a small number of songs get a rating, but every now and then a really popular tune will contain some words that are not appropriate for kids—and you don't want to be caught singing them at school. Songs like this are marked with a black-and-white Parental Advisory Label or by the word "explicit." The warning label appears on the packaging of the CD or next to a song listing if you buy it online.

If you see a song or album with this label, steer clear. Why? Because warnings are made to protect you from subjects that might make you—or your parents—upset. Besides, most popular songs with inappropriate lyrics also have a version labeled "clean"— exactly the same song with some words carefully blocked out. That way, you can enjoy the music without worrying about the bad stuff.

playlists and CDs

Online music collections make it easy to group songs into *playlists*, or lists of songs that you create based on certain themes. Try some of these:

Find high-energy songs that get you and your friends pumped up for a big basketball game or swim meet.

If you're driving to New York, find songs with "New York" in the title, and make a CD for your family to listen to in the car. If you're going to the ocean, play songs about surfing or the beach.

Ask members of your family for holiday songs they love. Then put those family favorites together on one CD, and play it during holiday get-togethers.

Find songs that calm you down or recordings of nature sounds. Play these when school feels over-whelming or you just want to relax.

Choose some Hawaiian music for a luau-themed birthday party, or play the soundtrack to a movie you'll watch during a sleepover.

music to your ears

Now hear this! It can be fun to blast music sometimes, but if you use headphones and turn up the tunes *too* high, you might damage your hearing. Look for "noise-canceling" headphones, which will protect your ears. And keep the volume turned down to medium.

Sometimes different songs in a playlist were recorded at very different volumes. You might have to turn up the volume to hear one song and turn down the volume when the next song comes on. To make sure your ears don't get damaged by an unexpectedly loud tune, keep the volume button within reach—and be prepared to adjust it as each new song begins.

making a difference

stay connected to family

Looking for more ways to reach out to family online? Try these:

Send an e-mail.
E-mail your grandparents or cousins once a week to stay in touch.
Pick a day when you have time to recap your week, and tell them
what's been going on in your life.

Look up your roots.
Did your distant relatives come from Ireland? Kenya? China?
Learn about the country of your great-great-great-grandparents
and its customs and climate.

IM your parents.
Add them to your buddy list and surprise them with an occasional
"hey." Teach them net lingo, such as TTYL ("Talk to you later").

Create a monthly newsletter.
Write a family newsletter that you e-mail every month to cousins,
grandparents, aunts, and uncles. Print out copies to send to family
members without e-mail.

Plan family trips.
Planning a road trip? Plot the distance on a map and find mini-golf
locations, weather forecasts, and fun highway stops along the way.

Send photos.
Help relatives across the country feel as if they are right there with
you for a birthday or a bike ride by sending pictures through e-mail.

Share Web sites.
Does your grandma love to knit? Does your older brother dig skiing?
When you find a cool Web site on a subject a family member loves,
copy the Web site address into an e-mail and pass it along.

boost your grades

How can you use the Internet to sharpen your study skills?

Look up ideas.
Need a project for the school science fair? Looking for a good topic for a research paper? When you're stumped, check the Internet for ideas.

Find homework helpers.
Stuck on a math problem? Look up the solution online by searching for "homework help." You'll find Web sites to help you with everything from math and science to history and language arts. Share your favorite sites with your teacher, who can share them with the class.

Get the facts.
When you're working on a project, use the Internet to find photos and fun facts to make your project more interesting—or to find books that will help you learn more.

Forgot your textbook at home?
Ask your teacher if any of your textbooks are available in digital form online. That way, if you forget your science book at school, you might be able to read it online and still get your homework done.

Take a class online.
Some schools offer classes online that you can't take in the classroom. Ask your teachers about opportunities to study different subjects or to get extra writing help online.

Practice quizzes.
Multiplication tables stumping you? Have to learn the state capitals? Look for timed quizzes and educational games online that make memorizing much more easy and fun.

Quiz yourself! Look for printable flash cards and other *School Smarts* activities at "Fun for Girls," americangirl.com.

Check your school Web site.
Most schools have a Web site that lists school schedules, events, and activities. Some classrooms even have their own Web sites where teachers list important dates and homework assignments. Check in regularly to keep up with what's going on.

E-mail your teacher.
If you've got a question about schoolwork or are concerned about something that happened in class, e-mail your teacher. Most teachers have their e-mail addresses printed in the school directory or on the school Web site.

help your community

Want to use the Internet to make a difference in your world?
Here's how:

Rescue an animal.
Visit the Web site of your local animal shelter to see what you can
do to help furry friends in need. Can you download a picture of an
animal that's up for adoption and post it in your neighborhood?

Save the planet.
Learn how to "go green" at environmental Web sites. Then
teach your whole family some new earth-friendly habits. Print
out recycling tips and post them near your family's trash containers.

Help a neighbor.
Go to the Web site of your city, village, or neighborhood association
and search under "volunteer." Talk to a parent about which projects
you can help out with in your community.

Feed the hungry.
Visit the Web site for a local food pantry, and look for a wish list of items the pantry needs most. Host your own mini food drive, and post information about it on a family blog or Web site.

Help other kids.
Find a local children's hospital or shelter that could use your gently used books, toys, and stuffed animals. E-mail your friends and ask if they'd like to donate, too.

Pitch in at your school.
Is your school planting a garden or raising money for a new piano? Visit the school Web site to find out. Then e-mail the teachers involved in the projects and ask how you can help.

have fun!

Make a difference in your own busy life by making time for fun. Looking for more ways to play online? Add these ideas to your list:

- Find a smoothie recipe.

- Visit a movie star's fan site.

- Check out this season's fashions.

- Love ponies or poodles? Learn more about your dream pet online.

- See your house from space! Or look up a live-camera view of a faraway place, such as Paris or London.

- Learn about a country you want to visit, such as Australia, Fiji, or Korea.

- Find a fun craft for your next sleepover.

- Look up movie reviews for the latest flicks.

- Search for cool party ideas for your next birthday.

- Find funny animal photos.

- Look for weekly sales at the local mall.

- Look up news from the year you were born.

- Read a biography about a person who inspires you.

- Find ideas for redecorating your room.

- Read book reviews.

- Check out new hairstyles to try.

- Play Sudoku.

- Find money tips, adopt a Net Pet, and play games at "Fun for Girls," americangirl.com.

That's it. And that's *a lot.* The Internet is the world—your friends, your family, and your interests—at your fingertips. And it's growing.

The Internet is always "on" and almost always easy to access, and it will always be up to you to make good choices about how you use it. As you get older, there will be even more to explore online. Practice your best habits now so that you'll be prepared when the time comes to explore more.

In the meantime, use these journal pages to jot down your favorite Web sites—places you get homework help, play games, and just have fun.

homework help

great games

great games

other fun sites

other fun sites

other fun sites